WiRES AND WATTS

WIRES AND WATTS

UNDERSTANDING AND USING ELECTRICITY

IRWIN MATH

aladdin books
MACMILLAN PUBLISHING COMPANY · NEW YORK
COLLIER MACMILLAN PUBLISHERS · london

I would like to express my thanks to Mr. Hal Keith for his excellent execution of the drawings for this book. I would also like to thank my son Robert and daughter Nicole for their interest and help in building and trying out most of the projects.

Additional thanks to Mr. Jerry Holzman of the Bronx High School of Science for his comments and suggestions, and especially to Mr. Charles Scribner, Jr., and to my editor, Ms. Clare Costello, for their enthusiastic support.

I. M.

Aladdin Books
Macmillan Publishing Company
866 Third Avenue, New York, NY 10022
Collier Macmillan Canada, Inc.
First Aladdin Books edition 1989
Printed in the United States of America
A hardcover edition of *Wires & Watts* is available from Charles Scribner's Sons, Macmillan Publishing Company.
10 9 8 7 6 5 4 3 2 1

Library of Congress Cataloging-in-Publication Data
Math, Irwin.
Wires and watts; understanding and using electricity/ Irwin Math.
         p.   cm.
Reprint. Originally published: New York: Scribner, © 1981.
Bibliography: p.
Includes index.
Summary: Uses experiments and projects that produce actual working models to present the fundamentals of electricity and magnetism.
ISBN 0-689-71298-7
1. Electricity—Juvenile literature. 2. Electricity—Experiments—Juvenile literature. [1. Electricity—Experiments. 2. Experiments.] I. Title.
[QC527.2.M37 1989]
537—dc19   88-7885   CIP   AC

To Ellen,

who is my source of Power

CONTENTS

List of Illustrations   ix
Foreword   xiii
Electrical Symbols Used in This Book   xv

1
WHAT IS ELECTRICITY?   1
Brief History . . . Pioneers . . . Static and Current Electricity
. . . Relationship to Magnetism

2
LET'S GET DOWN TO BASICS   7
What is Voltage? . . . Current? . . . What is a Circuit? . . . AC
and DC

3
SOURCES OF ELECTRICITY FOR THE
EXPERIMENTER   15
Batteries . . . Series and Parallel . . . Transformers . . . The
AC Power Line

4

MEASURING ELECTRICITY   24
Compass Indicator . . . Resistance . . . Voltage/Current
Indicator

5

TOOLS OF THE TRADE   31
Wire . . . Switches . . . Connection Methods . . .
Recommended Tools

6

POWER AND LIGHT   37
Heaters . . . Watts . . . Building a Lamp . . . Soldering . . .
Dollhouse Project . . . Emergency Lighting

7

MAGNETISM AND ELECTROMAGNETS   46
Model Railroad Semaphore . . . Electromagnetic Relay . . .
Buzzer

8

THE ELECTRIC MOTOR   53
How it works . . . How to build one . . . Uses

9

ALARMS   59
Basic Principles . . . Simple Protection Schemes . . .
Complete Burglar Alarms

10

FUN AND GAMES   63
Steady Hand . . . Pokerino . . . Speed of Response . . .
River-Crossing Puzzle

For Further Reading   71
Index   73

list of illustrations

1. A Charged Comb Readily Picks Up Small Bits of Paper or Cork
2. Construction Details of Compass-Type Current Detector
3. An Ultra-Simple Lemon Battery
4. Demonstration of Michael Faraday's Famous Experiment
5. Water Pipe Analogy
6. Flashlight Circuit
7. Complete-Circuit Experiment
8. Insulator/Conductor Tester
9. Cutaway View of Two Common Dry Cells
10. Multiple-Cell Batteries
11. Simple "Wet" Cell
12. Generator Experiment
13. Comparison of Direct and Alternating Current Flow
14. Simple Battery Holder for D Cells
15. Connecting Batteries in Parallel
16. Current-Measuring Experiment: Initial Hookup
17. Completion of Current-Measuring Experiment

18. *Series-Connected Batteries*
19. *An Experimenter's DC Power Supply*
20. *Construction Details of DC Power Supply*
21. *Parts of a Common Transformer*
22. *Construction Details of AC Power Supply*
23. *The Three Versions of Ohm's Law*
24. *A Voltage/Current Indicator*
25. *Component Parts of Voltage/Current Indicator*
26. *Winding Details of Coil*
27. *Voltage Scale*
28. *Current-Calibration Setup*
29. *Completed Voltage/Current Scale*
30. *Typical Wires and Their Major Specifications*
31. *Common Wire Found in the Home and Most Hardware Stores*
32. *Readily Available "Knife" Switches*
33. *Several Types of Switches that Can Be Fabricated by the Experimenter*
34. *Several Methods for Joining Wires*
35. *Common Hand Tools*
36. *Production of Light by Means of an Electrical Current*
37. *Comparison of Edison's First Lamp with a Modern Incandescent Type*
38. *Some Common, Easy-to-Obtain Lamps and Sockets*
39. *Ceiling Fixtures*
40. *Method of Building a Floor Lamp*
41. *How to Solder*
42. *Parallel Connection of Lamps*
43. *Series – Parallel Combinations for Lamps of Different Voltages*
44. *A Typical Relay*
45. *Details of the Emergency Lighting System*
46. *A Simple Electromagnet Readily Picks Up Small Nails, Pins, Paperclips*
47. *Electromagnetic Sounder*
48. *Model Railroad Semaphore Signal*
49. *Homemade Electromagnetic Relay*
50. *"Latching Relay" Circuit*
51. *Converting the Relay to a Buzzer*
52. *Comparison of a Commercial Buzzer and Bell*
53. *Construction Details of a Solenoid*

54. Simple Electromagnetic Lock
55. Combination Lock Switch
56. Two Electromagnets Attract when Connected with the Proper Polarity
57. Electromagnet Support Details
58. Armature Preparation
59. Wiring of Commutator Sections
60. Assembly of Electric Motor
61. Contacting Strips and Overall Motor Wiring Diagram
62. The Simplest Burglar Alarm that Can Be Built
63. How to Install the Burglar Alarm Switch
64. Some Sensors that Break a Circuit
65. Closed-Circuit Burglar Alarm
66. "Steady Hand" Test of Skill
67. Pokerino Game
68. Schematic Diagram of Pokerino
69. Construction Details for Pokerino
70. Reaction Testing Device
71. Wiring Diagram of Reaction Tester
72. Construction Details of Reaction Tester
73. Farmer/River Puzzle
74. Schematic Diagram of Puzzle

foreword

During the first half of the twentieth century American youngsters seemed never to be bored. They built clubhouses, model cars, airplanes, and electrical and electronic devices of all kinds. Many were reasonably adept at figuring out how things worked without the benefit of specific instructions.

When one looks at the various playthings available to young people today, one is amazed by the incredible technical sophistication of the devices: electronic games, remote-controlled robots, dolls that walk and talk, and a host of electromechanical devices. The addition of a few C or D cells promises all sorts of entertainment. But something is missing. The user is relegated to the role of button-pusher and observer. There is not much to do in a creative sense and boredom quickly sets in. Even the "do-it-yourself" kit simply instructs the builder to put part A into hole A and part B into hole B, and so on. The principles of operation are omitted or passed off in a sentence or two.

This book is an attempt to rekindle the creative spirit, to teach the fundamentals of electricity and magnetism through experiments and projects that produce actual working models. Common, easily obtained, inexpensive materials are used. The working models are designed to function not only as independent devices but as building blocks for more elaborate devices. Working with batteries, switches, and lamps, for example, leads the experimenter to a complete dollhouse lighting system, which is then further developed into a home emergency lighting scheme that operates automatically during power failures.

It is the author's hope that this book will help spark a return to the kind of creative thinking that has been gone for too long.

I. M.

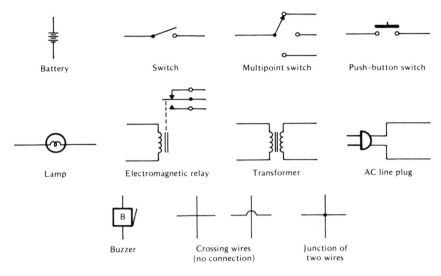

Electrical symbols used in this book.

WIRES AND WATTS

CHAPTER 1

WHAT IS ELECTRICITY?

The simple act of flicking a switch to turn on a lamp in a dark room is the result of thousands of years of scientific investigation and experimentation. The wondrous power of electricity that lights and heats our homes, operates complex machinery, and produces convenience and entertainment for millions of people, had its beginnings over 2000 years ago in ancient Greece. There, a scientist by the name of Thales of Miletus, born in 640 B.C., observed an unusual property of amber, a plastic-type material commonly used for jewelry. When rubbed briskly with fur, pieces of amber (or "elektron" as it was called) would attract small bits of cork, wood, or similar objects in much the same way that a magnet attracts metallic objects. Not understanding why this occurred, Thales assumed that some unknown force was present in the amber. This force came to be known as electricity.

Duplicating these early observations is quite easy to do with a plastic or hard rubber comb, to take the place of the amber, and a warm,

FIGURE 1

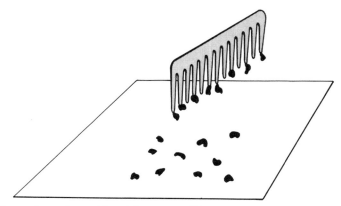

A charged comb readily picks up small bits of paper or cork.

dry, flannel cloth. Holding the comb in one hand and the cloth in the other, briskly rub the comb a dozen times or so. Now bring the comb near some small bits of paper or cork and the pieces will "jump" to the comb (see figure 1). This simple experiment, so many years ago, started it all—but it was a slow start!

Until the 18th century, experiments that were not much more involved than the one we just performed, were the extent of man's knowledge of electricity. While many observations were actually made and theories proposed, nothing of a really practical nature resulted. What did happen, however, was the formation of the general opinion that electricity is the action of subatomic particles called electrons. When these electrons are collected in abundance, as when the comb is rubbed, static electricity is produced and the comb is said to be "charged with electrons." If the electrons are made to continuously flow through a wire, current, or moving electricity, is produced. It is this second form that operates our modern world and is the form that we will be concerned with.

It was not until 1791 that practical progress began. In that year an Italian surgeon, Luigi Galvani, noticed that the legs of a frog he was experimenting with twitched every time he touched them with copper and zinc instruments. He had noticed a similar result when exposing the frog to a strong static electric "charge," so he concluded that the action had something to do with "electricity trapped in the frog." Although this conclusion was obviously wrong, Galvani's work made other scientists aware of this unusual occurrence. A few years later, in 1800, another Italian, Allesandro Volta determined what had actually happened to Galvani's frog. Volta found that an entire new form of electricity was produced whenever two dissimilar metals were brought in contact with each other in the presence of a strong, usually corrosive, liquid. The copper and zinc instruments of Galvani were the metals and the body fluid of the frog was the "corrosive" liquid. The leg muscles of the frog were simply acting as the detector of this new discovery, which Volta called current electricity. Further experimentation led him to produce the first true source of continuous current-electricity—the battery!

It is generally accepted that the work of Allesandro Volta was the single step that moved mankind into the modern world of electricity. The battery that he created clearly demonstrated that electricity could be produced on a continuous basis. The electrical unit of pressure, the "volt," was named in his honor.

To see how Volta's discovery actually worked, we require several easy-to-obtain items. First, we need two dissimilar metals such as copper and steel. The copper can be common electrical wire and the steel, a short length of coat-hanger wire. Be sure to use solid wire and remove any insulation, covering, or paint so that both wires are bright and clean. This can easily be done with sandpaper or file. For our "corrosive" liquid, a fresh lemon cut in half will do nicely. Finally, we will need a detector, and this we will have to build.

Figure 2 shows construction details of a simple detector that is inexpensive, easy to fabricate, and quite sensitive. All that is necessary is a Boy Scout-style compass, 25–30 feet of thin insulated copper wire, a couple of 6-32 by 1 1/2-inch-long machine screws and nuts, and two small pieces of wood. The wire should be between #24 and #30 gauge and can be obtained from an electrical supply house, old radio loudspeaker transformer, or, in a pinch, even from a telephone company

FIGURE 2

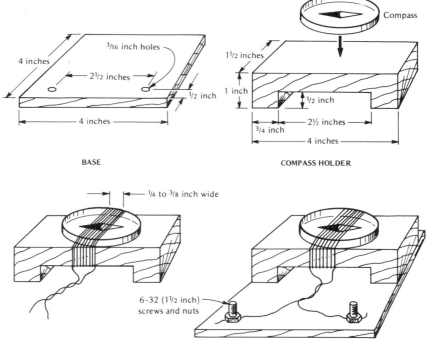

Construction details of a compass-type current detector.

installer who often uses such wire in his work. The wire must be insulated, except for 1/2-inch at each end. Use sandpaper, a file, or a knife to scrape away the insulation.

To begin construction, cut the two pieces of wood as shown in the figure. Then glue the compass to the U-shaped piece of wood, wind the wire around the wood and compass carefully, and secure it in place by twisting the leads as shown. Now glue the compass assembly to the base and connect the two leads to the machine screw "terminals." Finally, coat the wire turns with a thin layer of shellac or varnish to hold them permanently in place, and the detector is finished.

Now let's duplicate Volta's discovery. Referring to figure 3, push

FIGURE 3

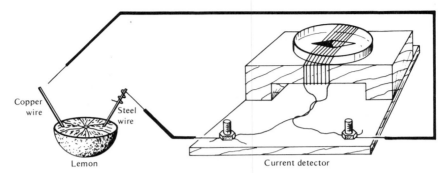

Copper wire

Steel wire

Lemon

Current detector

An ultra-simple lemon battery demonstrating Volta's famous discovery.

the steel and copper wires a short distance into the lemon. Connect one wire (called a lead) from the compass detector to the steel wire and hold the other detector wire in your hand. Orient the compass so that the pointer is parallel to the turns of wire and allow it to come to rest. Now, touch the detector lead to the copper wire in the lemon and see what happens to the compass. The violent movement indicates the production of current electricity. If you have a pair of earphones, connecting them to the lemon-battery will produce loud clicks as well.

Volta's original battery worked on this same exact principle. The only difference was that he used copper and zinc disks and, sandwiched between the disks, paper that had been soaked in saltwater.

The effect of Volta's discovery on the scientific world was immediate. At last, scientists had a continuous source of electricity to work with and progress was rapid. In 1819, a Danish scientist, Hans Christian Oersted, discovered that there was a direct relationship between electricity and magnetism by observing that a compass needle would move when brought near a wire in which an electrical current was flowing—just like our compass detector. Shortly thereafter, Michael Faraday proved that electricity could be converted into magnetism and vice versa by a famous and important experiment that we can easily repeat. Figure 4 shows the experiment.

On a 1/4-inch by 6-inch steel or iron spike—for example, a large

FIGURE 4

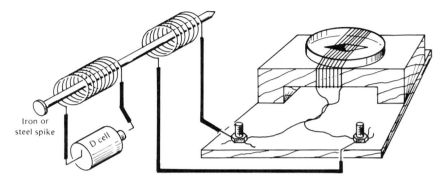

Iron or
steel spike

Demonstration of Michael Faraday's experiment.

nail that can be obtained from most lumber yards or building supply shops—wind two coils of about 20 turns each of common bell wire, leaving a 2-inch space between the coils. Connect one of the coils to the compass detector and the other to a D cell as shown.

If you alternately interrupt the battery circuit, by rapidly touching one of the wires to the battery terminal and then removing it, you will notice that the compass needle jumps back and forth. The current flowing in the coil connected to the battery causes the iron nail to become magnetized. The magnetic field then travels through the nail and acts on the second coil, where it is converted back into an electrical current. This experiment demonstrates the principles that led other scientists to the development of the transformer, generator, and electric motor a short time thereafter.

During the last half of the 1800s, many of the laws regarding current electricity were formulated, and by the early 1900s, the age of electricity had been established.

CHAPTER 2

let's get down to basics

Although no one has ever seen electricity, learning to use it properly need not be difficult. Understanding a few basic principles can make the difference between the successful experimenter and the disappointed amateur. Let us begin with a few facts that will be useful in our future experimenting.

Always remember that electricity flows—just like a liquid. The flow of electricity through a wire can be compared to the flow of water through a pipe. If you drilled a hole in the side of a pipe (figure 5) and

FIGURE 5

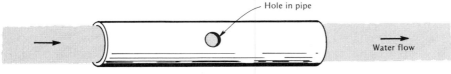

Hole in pipe

Water flow

Water pipe analogy.

looked in, you would see that a certain amount of water was passing your viewing point each second, producing a water current like the current in a river. Stick your finger in the hole in the pipe and you will feel the pull, or strength, of the current. This strength is determined by how much force or pressure is being applied at the end of the pipe.

A wire with electricity flowing through it has similar characteristics. The flow of electricity is called electric current. The strength of this current is also determined by the amount of pressure applied to the wire—in this case, electric pressure.

In the water system, the current is measured in gallons moving through a cross section of pipe per second. Pressure is measured in pounds per square inch. Electric current is measured in units called amperes and pressure is measured in volts. In either system, the higher the pressure, the greater the current.

It is not enough for an electric current to flow to have pressure (voltage) available. The current must flow in a complete path, or circuit, from its source through wires and other components, and back to the source. A break in the circuit will stop the flow.

Figure 6 shows a simple electric circuit where the current flows from the battery through the switch (when it is closed), through the light bulb, and back to the battery. If you break the circuit by opening the switch, or if there is a break in the wires, the flow of current will stop

FIGURE 6

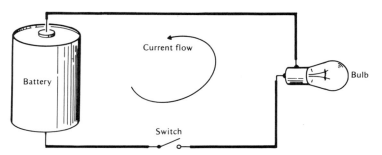

Flashlight circuit. This is the basic circuit used in most flashlights and lanterns.

FIGURE 7

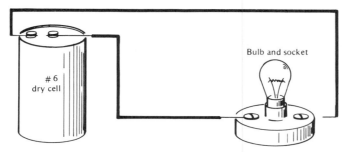

Complete circuit experiment. Be sure to remove insulating covering from wire.

and the bulb will go out. When a light bulb burns out (by a break in the filament) the circuit inside the bulb has been interrupted.

Whether the circuit is a simple flashlight or a complicated hookup from an electric power station to your home, the circuit must be complete, which is why the power cord connected to a home appliance has at least two wires, one for incoming flow, the other for outgoing flow.

A simple experiment will demonstrate this. A few common items, which are easy to obtain, are needed: a #6 dry cell; a piece of common bell wire; a #222 flashlight bulb; and a matching socket from your hardware store. Carefully remove some covering from each end of two 12-inch lengths of wire and hook up the circuit shown in figure 7. Connect one wire to the battery. The bulb will not light because there is no complete path. Now connect the open wire to the remaining screw on the socket, and the bulb will light.

Electric current will only flow through certain materials called conductors. Almost all metals, particularly copper (the metal most wires are made of), are good conductors. A material that electricity cannot flow through is called an insulator. The covering on the wire used to hook up the light-bulb circuit is an insulator. It is used to keep the current inside the wire and prevent it from flowing to adjacent wires if the wires accidentally touch.

The light-bulb circuit can easily be modified to help us learn about

FIGURE 8

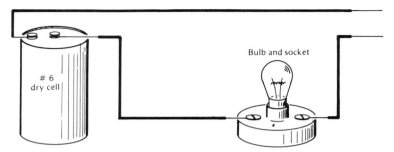

Insulator/conductor tester. With this simple device you can check the conductivity of most materials. You can also use it to be sure that electrical connections have been properly made.

which materials are conductors and which are insulators. Cut another 12-inch length of wire and reconnect the circuit (figure 8). The bulb will not light with the two wires unconnected. If a conductor of electricity is placed between the wires, the circuit will be completed and the bulb will light. Using this simple conductivity tester, we can experiment with glass, plastic, wood, rubber, and various metals to determine which are conductors and which are insulators.

FIGURE 9

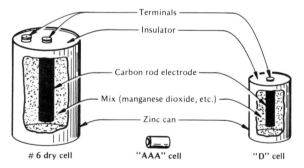

Cut-away view of two common dry cells (carbon–zinc types). All produce 1.5 volts. At a current of 1/10 ampere, the # 6 cell will last 550 hours, the D cell 50 hours, and the tiny AAA cell only 1½ hours.

Not all conductors are metals. Liquids such as water can also conduct electricity. To see this, place the two wires from the tester in a glass of water. Water is a conductor, but its degree of conduction is too low to light the bulb. Now add 1–2 tablespoons of salt to the water. The dissolved salt increases conduction to the point where the bulb will light.

The battery in our experiment has a pressure of only 1.5 volts. If the voltage is much higher than a small battery can supply (for example, the 115 volts from a household outlet), plain water can not only light a bulb but shock and even seriously injure a person standing in a puddle of water if that person touches a faulty electric appliance.

Electricity can be produced in many ways. The experimenter often uses the common dry-cell battery (shown cut apart in figure 9), consisting of a carbon rod, a zinc can, and a moist chemical filler. It is the interaction of these components that produces electricity. A carbon–zinc dry cell has a voltage of 1.5 volts regardless of its size, whether it is our #6 cell, the familiar D cell, or a tiny AAA penlight cell. But the large #6 cell will deliver almost 75 times as much current as the AAA cell. In a fixed current application, such as keeping a lamp lit, the larger battery will do the job longer.

Many cells can be connected together to produce high-voltage bat-

FIGURE 10

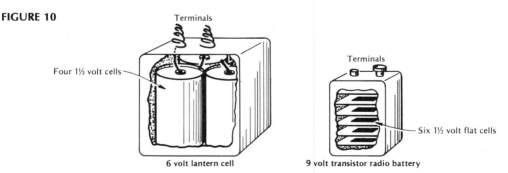

Multiple cell batteries. In batteries such as these, single cells are connected together to form higher voltage units.

FIGURE 11

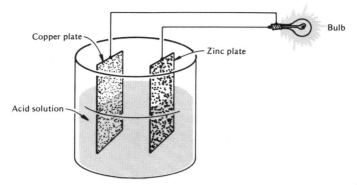

Copper plate

Zinc plate

Acid solution

Bulb

Simple "wet" cell. Most dissimilar metals will produce electricity.

teries (figure 10). In fact, the term "battery" really means two or more cells that have been connected together.

Wet-cell batteries such as the lead–acid battery used in automobiles (see simplified form in figure 11) are common. The electricity in a lead–acid battery is produced by the action of an acid–water mixture on two plates, each made of a different metal. Other chemical batteries may use different metals, alkaline mixtures, and so on, but the common fault remains: after a while the chemicals are used up, to the point that voltage and current decrease and make the battery useless. This is why batteries are only useful for relatively short-lived applications, as when current from a stationary source is unavailable.

Where continuous power is needed, as in homes, schools, and factories, the method used to produce electricity is based on the fact that magnetic energy and electric energy are easily converted to each other.

To illustrate this we need a bar magnet of the kind supplied with some children's games and our current detector of figure 2.

Referring to figure 12, make a coil of 10 turns of ordinary bell wire approximately 1 1/2 to 2 inches in diameter and connect it to the current detector. Now move the bar magnet quickly in and out of the "generator coil." The compass needle will deflect each time you move the magnet, proving that an electric current is flowing. The moving magnet

FIGURE 12

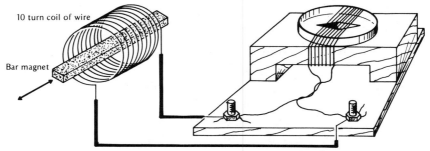

Generator experiment. Moving the bar magnet in and out of the coil produces a current that is detected by the compass needle.

is converting magnetic energy into electric energy, which flows through the connecting wires to the detector. There, it is converted back into magnetic energy and deflects the compass needle.

If you were paying close attention, you noticed that when you moved the magnet into the coil the compass deflected in one direction. When you then pulled the magnet out of the coil, the needle moved in the opposite direction. What actually happened was that the current first flowed in one direction, then in the other. If a source of mechanical power were hooked up to move the magnet in and out of the coil continuously, the current that would flow would reverse, or alternate, in the

FIGURE 13

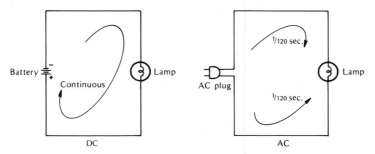

Comparison of direct and alternating current flow. The AC in our homes reverses 120 times per second.

same manner. Such a current is called an alternating current (or AC) and is the type that is supplied at the electrical outlets in our homes. Its direction of flow reverses at the rate of 120 times per second. Current produced by a battery is called direct current (or DC), since it only flows in one direction. Figure 13 summarizes both DC and AC current characteristics.

By means of other sources of power, such as water or steam, huge magnets are moved in close proximity to huge coils of wire, generating large amounts of alternating current in special generating stations owned and operated by the major electrical power companies. These generators operate as long as external mechanical power is applied to them. This is how we obtain the continuous energy required by our society.

CHAPTER 3

SOURCES of ELECTRICITY for THE EXPERIMENTER

To learn more about electricity, we will, of course, have to perform many experiments, and all of these will require a source of electrical current. We have already seen how the first battery was made and the principles behind the modern generator, but neither of these in the forms described is suited to our needs. We require a source of DC and AC current that we can use (and abuse) with relative safety and one that will also supply adequate power for our projects.

There are two choices. One is common dry-cell batteries and the other, a low-voltage version of the normal AC power line in our homes. Both of these will be discussed and complete power sources, suitable for the most experimental purposes, will be described.

As we have already seen in chapter 2, batteries come in all sizes and shapes. The one most suited to our needs is the #6, 1.5-volt "dry cell" unit. It has a high current capability and can tolerate a good deal of electrical misuse. Such batteries can be obtained from most hardware stores, but they tend to be somewhat expensive, particularly for the experimenter on a limited budget. If cost is a factor, try visiting a local company that installs and maintains burglar alarms. Such companies use #6 batteries by the dozen and usually have a quantity of "slightly used" batteries available that will often be given to the experimenter who simply asks. In almost all cases these batteries have been removed from service for reliability purposes. They still have plenty of reserve capacity, however, and will suit the experimenter perfectly.

If you are not lucky enough to be able to obtain the batteries you

FIGURE 14

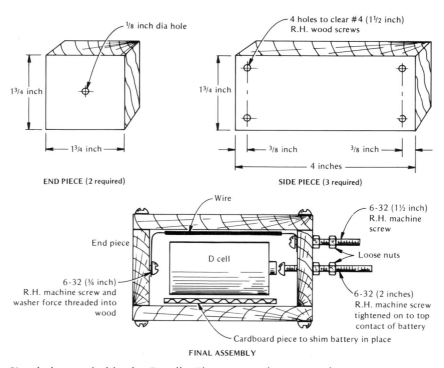

Simple battery holder for D cells. The nuts on the top machine screws are used to clamp external wires.

require, common D cells can be used with good results, although they will become exhausted faster than the larger ones.

The batteries we will be using all have an electrical pressure or potential of 1.5 volts. The current-producing capability, however, is a function of the size of the actual unit. Typical #6 dry cells can supply continuous currents of as high as 1.5 amperes, while D cells can only produce about one-tenth that amount. Often, higher voltages or currents will be required for particular experiments, so a bit of knowledge as to how batteries may be interconnected to achieve different voltages and currents is in order.

Since doing is preferable to a simple written explanation, we will learn how to vary voltage and current with a few simple experiments. To do these will require four #6 or D cells, some ordinary bell wire, a compass, such as the one used in the current detector, and a 6-volt replacement lantern lamp with matching socket from the local hardware store. The #6 cells have screw terminals for easy connections, but the D cells do not. If you are using D cells, then four of the holders shown in figure 14 must be built. These are quite simple and should pose no problems. After assembling the holders, drop a D cell into each as shown, wedge it in place with cardboard, then tighten the center screw, and you are ready to experiment. It is advisable at this time to test the holder by connecting a #222 lamp across the two terminal screws. If the lamp lights, the holder is functioning properly.

Referring back to the water concept of chapter 2, let us think of a battery as a tank of electrons under pressure, much like the liquid in a common aerosol can. The larger the can, the more liquid available (current capacity), but the pressure of the propelling gas (voltage) is the same regardless of size. A small can will therefore use up its contents quicker than a larger one, even though the pressure is the same. How then do we increase the current? Simple—just add another can. Figure 15 shows how this is done with batteries and pressure cans. Such a connection is known as a parallel circuit. The two batteries are said to be in parallel and the current capacity is now equal to the sum of the current capacities of each individual battery. To demonstrate this, hook

FIGURE 15

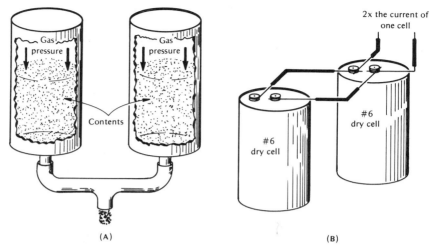

Connecting batteries in parallel increases the current capability just as connecting aerosol cans together increases the amount of contents available.

up the circuit shown in figure 16. Orient a compass so that the needle is parallel to the wire and about 2 inches away from it. Now connect the free wire to the battery just long enough to see how far the compass

FIGURE 16

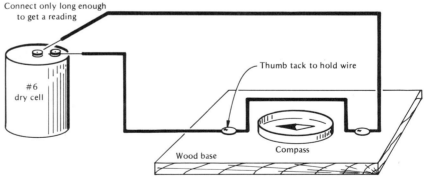

Current-measuring experiment: initial hookup.

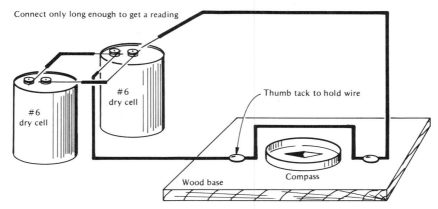

FIGURE 17 Connect only long enough to get a reading

#6 dry cell

#6 dry cell

Thumb tack to hold wire

Compass

Wood base

Completion of current-measuring experiment.

needle deflects. Move the compass closer or farther away from the wire until the deflection is just enough to clearly see—a movement of about 1/16 inch is fine. Now connect a second battery in parallel with the first, and again momentarily connect the free wire to the battery. The compass needle will deflect approximately twice as far, indicating the increased current capacity of the two batteries (figure 17). Do not leave any of these circuits connected longer than is necessary to notice the amount of deflection of the compass needle. The drain from the batteries is considerable and they will be exhausted in short order.

Similarly, you can increase the pressure or voltage of a group of batteries to enable more current to be pushed. This time, however, the batteries are connected in what is known as a series circuit. Figure 18 shows this configuration. To see the effect of such a circuit, first connect one battery to a 6-volt lantern lamp and notice how bright it lights. Now connect a second battery, then a third, and finally the fourth. Notice how the lamp gets brighter each time the voltage increases. This increase is due to more and more current being pushed through the lamp. If you do the same experiment with parallel batteries, you will see that the lamp remains at the same brightness regardless of how many bat-

FIGURE 18

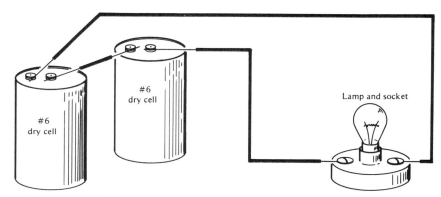

Series-connected batteries. Repeat this experiment with two, three, and four dry cells. Be sure to connect the batteries exactly as shown.

teries are added. Although in this case there is much more current available, there is not any more voltage to push it. In conclusion, then, connect batteries in parallel for more current capability and in series for more voltage.

Figure 19 is a drawing of an experimenter's DC power supply that will be of great convenience in future projects. It consists of four 1.5-volt batteries and a homemade switch allowing a selection of 1.5 through 6 volts to be achieved. The dimensions given will accommo-

FIGURE 19

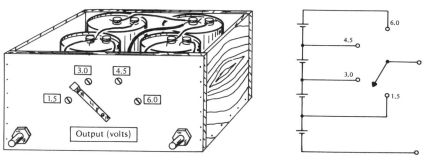

Drawing and circuit diagram of an experimenter's DC power supply.

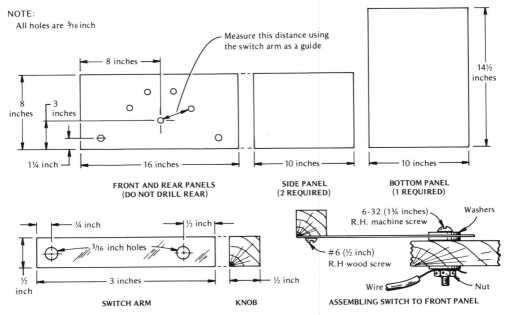

NOTE:
All holes are 3/16 inch

Measure this distance using the switch arm as a guide

8 inches

8 inches

3 inches

1¼ inch

16 inches

FRONT AND REAR PANELS
(DO NOT DRILL REAR)

10 inches

SIDE PANEL
(2 REQUIRED)

10 inches

BOTTOM PANEL
(1 REQUIRED)

14½ inches

¼ inch

½ inch

3/16 inch holes

½ inch

3 inches

½ inch

SWITCH ARM

KNOB

6-32 (1¾ inches) R.H. machine screw

Washers

#6 (½ inch) R.H wood screw

Wire

Nut

ASSEMBLING SWITCH TO FRONT PANEL

FIGURE 20   *Construction details of the DC power supply.*

date #6 cells; however, D cells can be used with the holders shown in figure 14. The switch mechanism is made of tin-can metal, and the switch contacts are arranged so that an "off" position is present between each contact for standby purposes.

Begin by cutting all of the wood—which, by the way, will almost always be a gift from the local lumber yard—and drilling the holes as shown in figure 20. Then cut the tin-can metal, file all sharp edges, and connect the wires as shown. Be sure all screws are tight and contacting surfaces clean of paint, varnish, or other insulation. For appearances, the wood may be stained and varnished before assembly.

Once the unit is built, it should be tested by connecting the 6-volt lantern lamp to the terminals. Moving the switch from one position to another should cause the lamp to get progressively brighter.

FIGURE 21

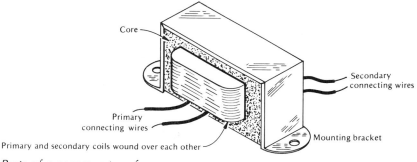

Core

Secondary connecting wires

Primary connecting wires

Primary and secondary coils wound over each other

Mounting bracket

Parts of a common transformer.

Producing AC for the experimenter is not much more complicated. Since generators are not easily built by experimenters, our power source will be derived from the household power line. To do this requires the use of a device called a transformer. As we have seen in the experiment of figure 4, a changing electric current in a coil around an iron core will produce a changing magnetic field in the core. This magnetic field will then produce another changing current in a second coil wound around the same core. This is the principle of the transformer and figure 21 is a representation of the type of unit that is most common. It consists of two coils, wound over each other, on a core made of iron strips. The use of concentric coils and strips instead of a solid core is a modern-day improvement for greater efficiency, but operation is exactly the same.

The coil that is the "input coil" is referred to as the primary and is designed to produce the proper-strength magnetic field with the incoming current. The "output coil," or secondary, is wound with just enough wire to produce the current and voltage desired. The ratio of primary-to-secondary turns determines the actual transformation. For example, a transformer with a primary of 1000 turns of wire and a secondary of 100 turns of wire will convert a 110-volt input to an 11-volt output. The unit we will employ in our AC power supply will be a 115–6-volt commercial unit with a current capacity of 3 amperes. This unit will supply all of the current required for our further experimentation.

Figure 22 shows the construction details of our AC power supply.

FIGURE 22

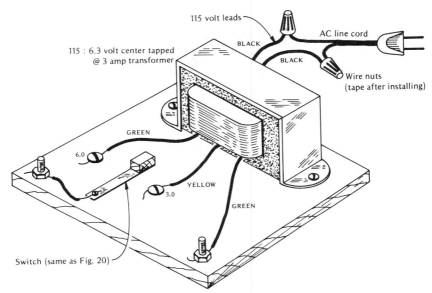

115 volt leads

AC line cord

BLACK

115 : 6.3 volt center tapped
@ 3 amp transformer

BLACK

Wire nuts
(tape after installing)

GREEN

6.0

YELLOW

3.0

GREEN

Switch (same as Fig. 20)

Construction details of an experimenter's AC power supply.

The transformer can be obtained at most electronic parts suppliers and should be of the type that has a "center-tapped secondary." This feature allows both 6 volts and 3 volts to be obtained. The switch, as in the DC supply, has a center position for "standby" use. When connecting the AC line cord to the primary of the transformer (the black wires), be absolutely certain that the connections are very well insulated. After connecting the wires securely, thread wire nuts (from the hardware store) over the twisted ends or terminals and then use black vinyl electrical tape over the wire nuts. The 115-volt pressure of the AC power line is quite high and can push enough current through a person to cause serious injury or at the least, a bad shock.

After completion, test the power source by connecting the 6-volt lamp to the terminals and moving the switch to its two positions. As a safety precaution, always unplug the line cord when not using the AC supply.

CHAPTER 4

MEASURING ELECTRICITY

Sooner or later, in one's pursuit of the mysteries of electricity, the need to measure voltage or current arises. Whether to check on the presence of current, the condition of a battery, or the continuity of a circuit, something beyond the simple "if-it-works-it's ok" approach is needed.

Fortunately the fabrication of several types of electrical measuring instruments is well within the capabilities of even the novice experimenter. In fact, we have already built two very useful devices—the tester of figure 8 and the compass indicator of figure 2. While neither of these will measure actual values, they will be found to be quite handy in our experimentation. While the tester of figure 8 was originally intended to determine if something was an insulator or conductor, it will be very useful as a tester of switches, wire connections, or the general continuity of electrical circuits. Likewise, the compass indicator is a sensitive detector of small amounts of current, much smaller indeed than that produced by the batteries we employ in our experiments. But indicators are not enough. If serious work is to be done we must have a way to actually measure voltage and current values.

First, however, there is one electrical quantity in addition to voltage and current that we must understand and this is resistance. We already know that voltage is required to push current through a circuit, but the amount of current that can be pushed is also a function of the circuit itself. Just like water pipes, large-diameter wires will allow a lot of current to flow and small, fine wires will allow very little. The degree of conduction of any wire or complete electrical circuit, is known as its resistance. Resistance is expressed in units called ohms in honor of Georg Simon Ohm, a German scientist of the early 1800s. Ohm discovered a relationship between volts and amperes that has been the primary law or rule of electricity since serious work began. This rule is known as Ohm's Law. It states, very simply, that the resistance of a circuit is equal to the voltage applied to the circuit divided by the resulting current that flows. In simple mathematical terms, $R = V/I$. A lamp that has 6 volts applied and requires 2 amperes to light has a resistance, therefore, of 3 ohms. If you reduce the voltage to 3 volts then only 1 ampere will flow since resistance is a constant factor. By rearranging the relationship of V, I, and R as shown in figure 23, any one of the three quantities or parameters can be determined if you know the other two. Therefore, you can first determine the resistance of a circuit, then accurately predict what will happen if you increase or decrease either voltage or current.

With this information in mind we can now proceed to figure 24, which shows an instrument that can be used to measure voltage or current. It is an adaptation of our compass indicator but can be calibrated and does not have to be oriented in any particular direction to operate. In principle, a magnet is moved in respect to the strength of the magnetic field that results from the current flow through a coil.

FIGURE 23 $V = I \times R$ $R = \dfrac{V}{I}$ $I = \dfrac{V}{R}$

The three versions of Ohm's Law.

FIGURE 24

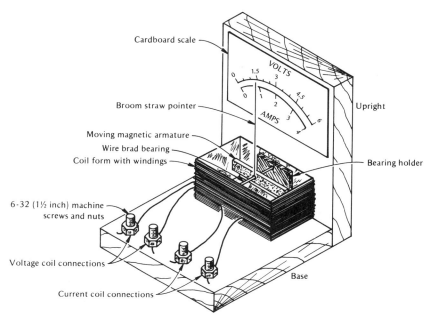

Cardboard scale

VOLTS

AMPS

Upright

Broom straw pointer

Moving magnetic armature
Wire brad bearing
Coil form with windings

Bearing holder

6-32 (1½ inch) machine
screws and nuts

Voltage coil connections

Current coil connections

Base

A voltage/current indicator that can be built by an experimenter.

In our indicator, however, there are two separate coils. One of these is wound with many turns of fine wire and exhibits high resistance to current flow. This coil will be used as a voltage sensor since large variations in voltage are necessary to vary the resulting magnetic field. The other coil is wound with just a few turns of heavy wire and has a very low resistance. This coil will be used as a current sensor.

Begin construction by cutting all of the wooden pieces to size as shown in figure 25(A). Then cut all the metal pieces and drill the necessary holes as in figure 25(B). Be certain to use a file to smooth all rough edges. Glue a small piece of a magnet from a toy on the armature as shown and press and glue a 16-gauge 1 1/2-inch-long wire brad through the center of the armature. Cut off both ends of the brad so the total length is 1 1/4 inch. Finally, glue a broom straw or very thin piece of wire to the armature to act as a pointer.

Now arrange the base and armature assembly as shown in figure

FIGURE 25

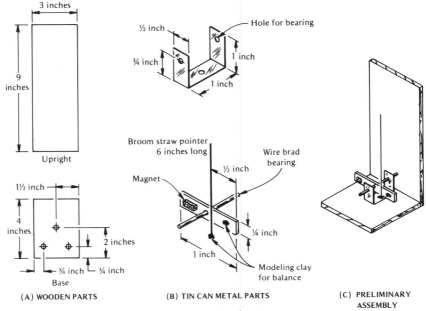

3 inches

9 inches

Upright

½ inch

¾ inch

Hole for bearing

1 inch

1 inch

1½ inch

4 inches

2 inches

¾ inch   ¾ inch

Base

(A) WOODEN PARTS

Broom straw pointer
6 inches long

Magnet

½ inch

Wire brad
bearing

¼ inch

1 inch

Modeling clay
for balance

(B) TIN CAN METAL PARTS

**(C) PRELIMINARY
ASSEMBLY**

Component parts of the voltage/current indicator.

25(C) and counterbalance the magnet with modeling clay so that the broom-straw pointer points to where 0 will be on the meter scale. The armature should move freely in its holder and when gently pushed, should swing back to 0 on the scale with no binding or hesitation. A drop of light household oil on the bearing surfaces may be necessary and if so, should be applied very sparingly.

To make the combination sensing coil, first prepare a "form block" of wood as shown in figure 26. Smooth it with sandpaper and wrap 2 to 3 turns of white bond paper around it, securing the paper with cellophane tape. Wind 500 turns of the finest enamel-insulated copper "magnet wire" you can find around the coil form. This will be the voltage coil. Wire of #28 gauge or smaller is desired and usually can be obtained either from the windings of old radio transformers or a local electrical supply house. Wind the coil neatly and as evenly as possible. After the coil is complete, bring out 3 inches of each end for connec-

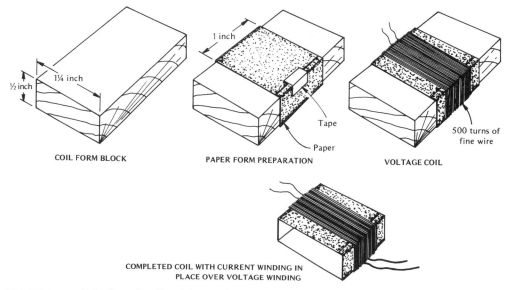

½ inch 1¼ inch

COIL FORM BLOCK

1 inch

Tape

Paper

PAPER FORM PREPARATION

500 turns of fine wire

VOLTAGE COIL

COMPLETED COIL WITH CURRENT WINDING IN PLACE OVER VOLTAGE WINDING

FIGURE 26   *Winding details of the coil.*

tions, and cover the whole assembly with three layers of black plastic electrical tape. Now wind 25 turns of common bell wire directly on the tape and then tape it in place. Finally, add a last layer of electrical tape over the complete coil and carefully slide the whole assembly off the form block. Be certain all windings are reasonably secure and coat the entire coil, inside and outside, liberally with shellac or varnish to give it additional strength.

When everything is dry, position the coil over the armature assembly and cement in place with common white glue. Neatly run the leads from the voltage coil and current coil to the correct terminals, as in Figure 24, and you are ready for calibration.

The voltmeter will be calibrated first. To begin, place the blank scale in position and attach the voltage sensing coil to one new, fresh #6 or D battery. Note where the pointer moves and place a mark on the scale in pencil. If the pointer moves in the wrong direction, reverse the battery leads. Next connect a second, then a third, and finally a fourth

FIGURE 27

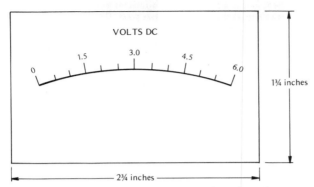

Voltage scale. Make all markings with India ink.

battery in series, always lightly marking the scale at 1.5-volt intervals. Remove the scale, and carefully copy the scale shown in figure 27. Use India ink, a thin felt-tip marker, or similar pen, to make a neat scale. Leave room, as shown, for the current scale.

Calibrating the current scale is a bit more involved. You will recall (Ohm's Law, stated at the beginning of the chapter) that by knowing the voltage and resistance of a circuit we can determine current. This is the method we will use for current calibration. You will need ten 10-ohm

FIGURE 28

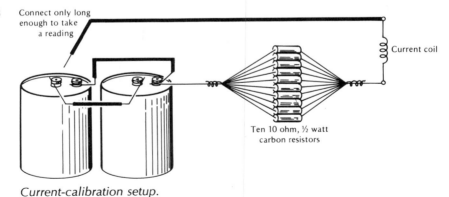

Current-calibration setup.

resistors from a local electronic or electrical supply shop. These should be the 1/2-watt carbon units and will usually cost about 5 cents each.

To begin, set up the circuit shown in figure 28. The ten 10-ohm resistors in parallel form the equivalent of a 1-ohm resistor, and with 3 volts across 1 ohm, a current of 3 amperes will flow. Mark this point on the scale. Remove 3 resistors, leaving a resistance of 1.4 ohms. Now slightly more than 2 amperes will flow, but you can mark this point on your scale as 2 amperes. Again remove resistors until only 3 resistors, or 3.33 ohms, are left. The current now is 0.9 amperes, almost 1. Mark this point as 1 ampere. Next mark 0.6 amperes (2 resistors) and 0.3 amperes (1 resistor).

Now remove the scale and ink in the finished scale and intermediate marks as shown in figure 29. This completes the calibration of the voltage/current indicator. If all construction procedures and calibration instructions have been carefully followed, you will have an accurate device that can be used in most of your future experimentation.

For those who wish to pursue the hobby of electricity seriously, the purchase of a commercial V-O-M (volt-ohm-meter) is highly recommended. This instrument has the advantage of measuring both AC and DC volts, amperes, and by means of an internal battery, ohms. If you do buy one, be sure that a good instruction manual is supplied with it. Such a "tool" is indispensable.

FIGURE 29

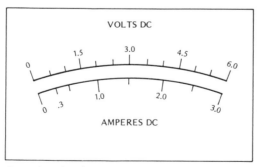

Completed voltage/current scale.

CHAPTER 5

TOOLS OF THE TRADE

At this point, the future experimenter will be starting to understand what electricity is all about. Voltage, current, resistance, circuits, etc., should no longer be just strange words. We are therefore ready to look at the components and tools that will be used to build, modify, and repair the working models we will be getting involved with.

Aside from the battery or other source of electricity, the most common item is, of course, the connecting wires. We already know that the larger the diameter of a wire, the more current it can accommodate, which is why electrical wire is manufactured in a wide range of sizes. Figure 30 shows some of the sizes likely to be encountered. All common electrical wire is manufactured of copper and is covered with a nonconducting coating referred to as insulation. The insulation prevents the loss of current if the wires come in contact with other bodies or themselves. Insulation is made of a wide range of materials that are intended for specific applications. Wires used for appliance power

FIGURE 30

WIRE SIZE	DIAMETER OF CONDUCTOR (INCHES)	MAXIMUM ALLOWABLE CURRENT (AMPERES)	TYPICAL USE
#10	.102	32.5	
#12	.081	23.0	General house wiring
#14	.064	16.2	
#16	.051	11.5	
#18	.040	8.1	Bells, buzzers, appliances
#20	.036	5.5	
#22	.025	4.0	
#24	.020	2.0	Electronic wiring
#26	.016	—	
#28	.013	—	
#30	.010	—	Transformers

Typical wires and their important specifications.

cords, for example, may be covered with rubber or rubberlike material for flexibility, whereas those used within the walls of houses have heavy, nonflammable plastic coatings. Underground wires often have similar plastic insulation that is further enclosed in lead or other metallic outer jackets. Wires intended for high-temperature use are usually insulated with ceramic beads, while those intended for use under water have heavy rubber coatings. The wire that the experimenter will find most convenient for his or her use will almost always have either plastic

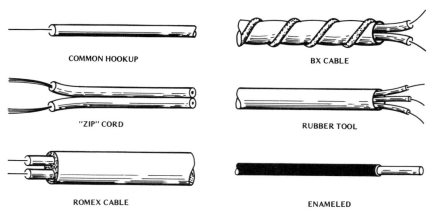

COMMON HOOKUP

BX CABLE

"ZIP" CORD

RUBBER TOOL

ROMEX CABLE

ENAMELED

FIGURE 31   *Common wire found in the home and at most hardware stores.*

FIGURE 32

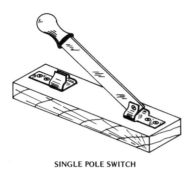
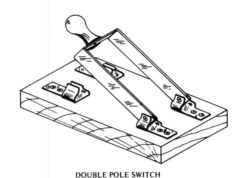

SINGLE POLE SWITCH   DOUBLE POLE SWITCH

Readily available "knife" switches.

insulation or a thin enamel coating and will have a solid or stranded copper conductor. The stranded wire is made to obtain greater flexibility—especially in the larger diameter conductors—and for most purposes is interchangeable with the solid type. Figure 31 shows some of the various types of wire in common use today.

Now that the circuit can be interconnected, it is desirable to be able to easily turn it on or off. This is the function of the switch. Very simply stated, a switch makes or breaks a circuit. The operation of the common knife switch, shown in figure 32 and available in most hardware stores, is obvious, and all switches, whether rotary, toggle, slide, or pushbutton, work in the same manner. Either there is a complete electrical path through them or there is not. Figure 33 shows several switches that can be made of wood, screws, and tin-can metal. All of these are suitable for use with the 6-volt DC or AC power supplies of chapter 3, but *should not be used directly with the AC power line* or serious electrical shocks may result.

There are a number of methods suggested for connecting wires to each other or to other parts of a circuit and these are shown in figure 34. When using methods (A) and (B), remove only enough insulation from the wire for the "twist." Then wrap plastic or vinyl electrical tape over the connection until no bare metal shows through. When using "wire nuts" (C), be sure they are the right size for the wire you are using. The

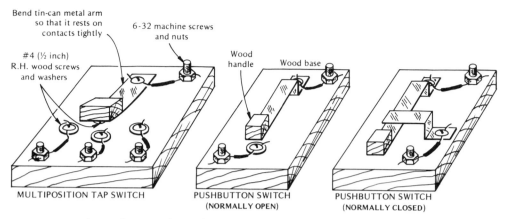

Bend tin-can metal arm
so that it rests on
contacts tightly

6-32 machine screws
and nuts

#4 (½ inch)
R.H. wood screws
and washers

Wood
handle

Wood base

MULTIPOSITION TAP SWITCH

PUSHBUTTON SWITCH
(NORMALLY OPEN)

PUSHBUTTON SWITCH
(NORMALLY CLOSED)

FIGURE 33 *Several types of switches that can be easily built by the experimenter.*

binding posts of figure 34(D) and (E) are self-explanatory and should always be securely tightened to make a good connection. The assembly shown in figure 34(F) is a "quick connect" post made of tin-can metal that will be useful for temporary hookups. In use, a wire is simply slid between the two metal strips. It should be clearly understood that the

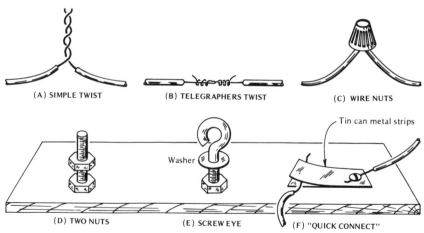

(A) SIMPLE TWIST   (B) TELEGRAPHERS TWIST   (C) WIRE NUTS

Washer

Tin can metal strips

(D) TWO NUTS   (E) SCREW EYE   (F) "QUICK CONNECT"

FIGURE 34 *Several methods for joining wires.*

FIGURE 35

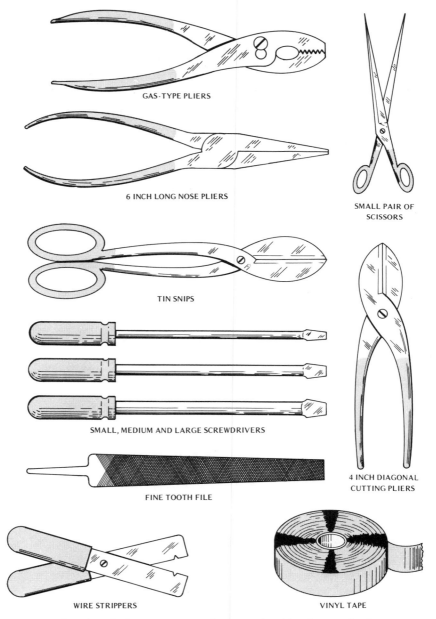

GAS-TYPE PLIERS

6 INCH LONG NOSE PLIERS

SMALL PAIR OF
SCISSORS

TIN SNIPS

SMALL, MEDIUM AND LARGE SCREWDRIVERS

4 INCH DIAGONAL
CUTTING PLIERS

FINE TOOTH FILE

WIRE STRIPPERS

VINYL TAPE

Common hand tools that every experimenter should strive to obtain.

object of all of the methods shown in figure 34 is to assure good metallic contact between all of the conductors involved. Be sure that there is no coating on the metal strips of the "quick connect" post.

General electrical experimentation will be made much easier and more enjoyable if the experimenter obtains some basic hand tools. These tools need not necessarily be expensive but should be of the best quality one can afford, so they will give long, reliable service—particularly with heavy usage.

If at all possible, the experimenter's tool complement should include:

1. Three slotted screwdrivers, one for use with #12 through 1/4-inch screws, one for use with #6 through #10 screws, and a fine blade screwdriver for use with #4 or smaller screws.

2. A pair of gas-type pliers.

3. A pair of 6-inch long nose pliers.

4. A pair of 4-inch diagonal cutting pliers.

5. A pair of wire strippers.

6. A small pair of scissors.

7. A 6–8-inch fine-tooth flat file.

8. An inexpensive pair of tin-snips.

9. A roll of black vinyl electrical tape.

Figure 35 shows examples of the type of tools that you should try to obtain. Optional items such as woodworking tools, a hand drill, and so on can be added as needed.

CHAPTER 6

POWER AND LIGHT

It is a well-known fact that energy can be converted from one form into another. A burning fire (chemical energy) can be used to boil water, producing steam, and the steam can be used to turn a turbine, thus producing rotary motion or mechanical energy. The rotating turbine can then be connected to a generator, thereby producing electricity. In a similar manner electrical energy can be converted into other forms of energy, and one of these is heat. When performing the experiments in the past chapters you may have noticed that at times, the connecting wires became warm to the touch. This indicated that just such a conversion was taking place within the wires.

Whenever voltage pushes current through a circuit, electrical energy is being produced. The actual amount of this energy is expressed in terms of watts, named in honor of James Watt, an 18th century inventor whose work made the steam engine a practical device. The number of watts can be determined by multiplying the voltage present by the current (in amperes) flowing. If we were to wind 20 turns of bell wire around a 1/2-inch-diameter wooden dowel, connect it to a 1 1/2-volt #6 dry cell, and find that 2 amperes of current flowed through the circuit, we would say that the circuit was consuming 1 1/2 × 2, or 3 watts. In this case, just about all of the energy would be converted into heat. In the common 100-watt light bulb, some of the 100 watts of power consumed is given off as light and some as heat.

The warm wires we just mentioned got warm as a result of the electrical energy overcoming the resistance of the wires. In fact, heat is produced whenever there is resistance in a wire or a circuit that must be overcome. This principle is basic to the workings of an entire group of common household products such as toasters, ovens, coffee machines, and even hair curlers. All of these contain special "heating element" wires made of nichrome, an alloy of nickel and chromium that presents a high electrical resistance to the passage of current. This wire is therefore a "good source of heat."

Keeping this idea in mind, we can see that when more and more current is pushed through a high-resistance wire, more and more heat will be produced. By continuing to increase the current, we eventually reach the point where so much heat is present that the wire actually glows and gives off light. This is the basis of the electric light. By way of illustration, try the following experiment. Secure two lengths of bell wire with thumb tacks to a piece of 2 × 4 lumber as in figure 36. Obtain a 6-inch length of a single strand of the wire used in a common power

FIGURE 36

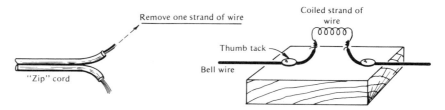

Production of light by means of an electrical current.

FIGURE 37

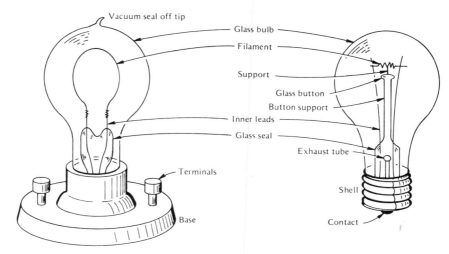

Vacuum seal off tip

Glass bulb

Filament

Support

Glass button

Button support

Inner leads

Glass seal

Exhaust tube

Terminals

Shell

Base

Contact

Comparison of Edison's first lamp with a modern incandescent type.

cord. You will have to cut apart an old power cord or ask for 6 inches of "zip cord" from your local hardware store. Wind the strand of wire around a small-diameter nail to produce a coil of wire and connect the free ends of this coil to the bell wire as shown.

Now hook up the entire circuit to your battery power supply. Apply 1 1/2 volts to the coil and watch what happens. The coil will heat up, and the close turns of high-resistance wire produce enough heat to glow. Increase the voltage to 3 volts and the coil will glow even brighter. Eventually this "electric light" will fail because the intense heat will weaken the wire and cause it to break. BE VERY CAREFUL WHEN DOING THIS EXPERIMENT. THE HEAT PRODUCED IS QUITE HIGH AND CAN CAUSE SERIOUS BURNS OR EVEN CAUSE PAPER TO BURN.

When Thomas Edison was developing a practical electric light he tried over 6000 different materials in an attempt to find one that would last. His first successful lamp, the result of all of that work, consisted of a fine (thin) filament of carbonized sewing thread mounted inside a glass bulb from which all of the air had been removed by means of a vacuum pump to prevent burning. This lamp lasted for about 40 hours. Additional work by scientists soon resulted in a filament made of a very rugged metal called tungsten. These lamps, essentially our lamps of today, operate for thousands of hours. Figure 37 is a drawing showing the parts of Edison's first practical lamp and a modern incandescent light bulb. Note the similarity between the two.

While household lamps are all intended for use at 115 volts, there is a wide range of lamps that are suitable for use with the AC and DC power supplies built in chapter 3. Figure 38 shows some of these, as well as inexpensive sockets that can be obtained for use with these lamps.

The use of these lamps offer interesting possibilities for the experimenter. One such unique application is the "electrification" of a doll house. By using the AC power supply of figure 22 and some of the lamps just mentioned, an entire dollhouse can easily be illuminated, thereby adding an exciting element of realism. The lamps used for this project should have brass bases. Since brass and aluminum are used interchangeably, be certain to get the correct ones.

When starting this project, one should first decide where the various lighting "fixtures" should be in each room. The most obvious place would be the ceiling, and figure 39 shows some of the types of fixtures

FIGURE 38

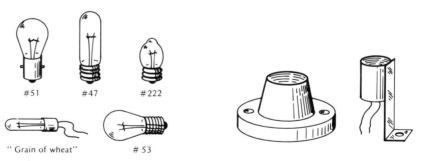

Some common, easy-to-obtain lamps and sockets.

FIGURE 39

Thin twisted wire "chain"

(A) PLASTIC TOOTHPASTE CAP
WITH LAMP GLUED IN END

(B) PING-PONG BALL WITH
LAMP GLUED IN END

(C) PLASTIC OR VINYL TUBE
WITH LAMP GLUED INSIDE

Several types of "ceiling fixtures" that can be made for an "electrified" dollhouse.

that can be fabricated from miniature lamps. In many cases, bottle caps, plastic tubing, and similar materials can be easily modified to serve as shades, and various colors will, of course, give different effects. Free-standing floor lamps and simulated floodlights can also be built as shown in figure 40.

Regardless of what type of fixture is finally decided on, it will be necessary to connect wires to the lamp itself. Because of space limitations, the best way to do this is by soldering the wires directly to the actual body of the lamp. If you are proficient in soldering, this will pose no problem. If you do not know how to solder and plan extensive elec-

FIGURE 40

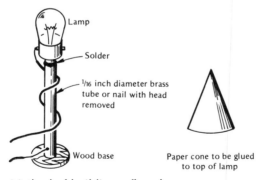
Lamp

Solder

1/16 inch diameter brass
tube or nail with head
removed

Wood base

Paper cone to be glued
to top of lamp

Small decorated
paper cup

Method of building a floor lamp.

FIGURE 41

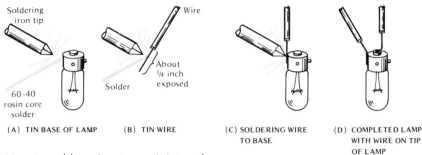

Soldering iron tip

Wire

60-40 rosin core solder

Solder

About 1/4 inch exposed

(A) TIN BASE OF LAMP   (B) TIN WIRE   (C) SOLDERING WIRE TO BASE   (D) COMPLETED LAMP WITH WIRE ON TIP OF LAMP

How to solder wires to a miniature lamp.

tric experimentation, soldering is a skill you must learn. With correct guidance, it won't take more than 15 minutes.

To solder wires to the lamp, look at figure 41. First touch a pencil-type soldering iron (30–50 watts) and 60–40 rosin core solder to the base of the lamp until a bit of the solder flows onto the brass base (figure 41(A)). Be certain it flows onto the brass and not the soldering iron. Then "tin" the end of one wire by holding it on the tip of the soldering iron with some solder until the solder melts around the wire (figure 41(B)). Now, touch the solder-clad wire to the bit of solder on the lamp base and heat both until the solder again melts (figure 41(C)). Remove the iron and let the joint cool. This completes one connection, and if done properly, the bond will be quite strong. To connect the other wire, again tin it. This time touch it to the solder ball at the tip of the lamp and heat both until the solder melts. Again remove the soldering iron, let the junction cool, and the job is finished (figure 41(D)). You might wish to test each lamp modified in this way to be certain that it is still working. Whenever soldering, BE CERTAIN TO ONLY USE ROSIN CORE SOLDER. ANY OTHER TYPE WILL CORRODE AND RUIN YOUR PROJECT.

Once the fixtures are made, they must be installed and wired. Ceiling fixtures may be hung from miniature screw eyes, floodlights mounted with bent nails or homemade brackets, and floor lamps secured in place by double-sided masking tape placed under the base. If

FIGURE 42

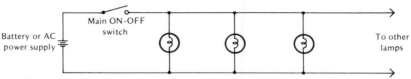

Parallel connection of lamps.

all lamps used are of the same voltage, then they can be connected in parallel as shown in figure 42. If they are of different voltages, then a series–parallel circuit must be used. Figure 43 shows such an arrangement. Here two 6-volt lamps and three 2-volt lamps are connected to a 6-volt battery. The 2-volt lamps are connected in series so that the total required voltage is 6 volts; this series "string" is connected in parallel with the two other 6-volt lamps. In this type of circuit usually only lamps of the same type can be connected in series for higher voltage use. A 2-volt and a 6-volt lamp cannot be properly connected for use at 8 volts because their internal resistance is different and the voltage applied to each lamp in such a circuit would not be correct. Switches can also be inserted at points in the circuit to enable various lamps to be turned on or off.

Another unique application of miniature lamps is a home emergency lighting system. In many homes, particularly those in rural areas, there are occasional power failures due to storms, winds, rains, etc.

FIGURE 43

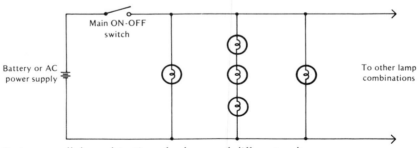

Series–parallel combinations for lamps of different voltages.

FIGURE 44

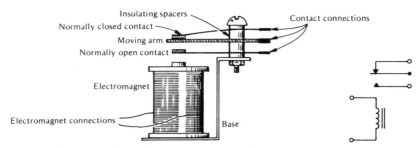

A typical relay and its schematic representation.

These failures often occur at night, plunging the house into darkness and causing a scramble to find a flashlight. The system to be described can change all of that!

In principle, an ideal emergency lighting system would turn on as soon as the power failed, then turn off when the power was restored. This is what our circuit does. The "sensor," which will have to be purchased from an electrical supply company, is a 115-volt AC SPDT electromagnetic relay or just "relay." Its operation is shown in figure 44. A coil, which becomes an electromagnet, is connected to the AC line. This electromagnet pulls on a set of contacts, breaking the circuit to a group of lamps distributed through the house. As long as AC is present,

FIGURE 45

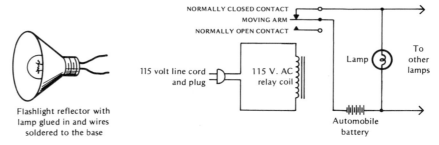

Lamp assembly details and final wiring diagram of the emergency lighting system.

the relay will keep the circuit nonconducting and all of the lamps will, of course, be off. When the power fails, however, the contacts close and the lamps come on.

For the lamp assemblies, use the reflectors from the most inexpensive flashlights you can find. These are fitted with #53 12-volt lamps, which can usually be obtained from the same source that you obtained the relay. The lamps are glued into the reflectors and the reflectors mounted near or in the ceiling, one to each room that is to be illuminated. For a power source, a used 12-volt automobile battery is employed, as it usually has more than enough current capacity to keep the lamps on for several hours. This battery can be the smallest available and is readily obtained for a couple of dollars at local service stations or automotive junk yards. When buying such a used device, you might wish to take a 12-volt lamp along for testing purposes. After you buy one, it is advisable to take it to an auto-mechanic shop for recharging.

Figure 45 shows the actual construction of the lamp assemblies and the overall final circuit. When installing such a system, use #16–#18 bell wire and try to be as neat as possible. The final installation should be practically unnoticeable. Now, when the lights go out, you will be prepared!

CHAPTER 7

MAGNETISM AND ELECTROMAGNETS

From the experiment performed in figure 4, we know that electrical energy can be converted into magnetic energy. Now it is time to put this fact to work for us.

On a 1/4 by 3-inch stove bolt, neatly wind 50 turns of bell wire as shown in figure 46. Connect the ends of this winding to a #6 dry cell and note how the magnetic energy produced in the bolt picks up small nails, paper clips, pins, etc. Such a device is an electromagnet and it is the basis of many electrical devices found in our daily lives. Now, refer to figure 47. Cut a wood base and a strip of tin-can metal and mount them along with the electromagnet in the manner shown. If you carefully bend and position the metal strip, you will find that every time you apply power to the electromagnet, the strip will move toward the bolt and strike it making an audible "click." When you remove power, the strip will move away due to the spring action of the metal. If this is not very obvious, increase the voltage to 3 volts (two batteries).

FIGURE 46

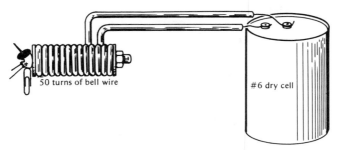

50 turns of bell wire

#6 dry cell

A simple electromagnet readily picks up small nails, pins, and paper clips.

It is interesting to note that this simple device was the basis of Samuel Morse's telegraph, which he began developing in 1832. By locating an electromagnetic sounder at one point and a switch at a distant point, the clicks of the unit could be controlled in accordance with a predetermined code with the result that messages could be sent between the two points.

We can utilize the movement of the metal strip in other ways, however. Figure 48 shows such a way. Here we have added a wooden support and semaphore flag cut from tin-can metal and produced a signal that is ideal for a model railroad. By careful construction and adjust-

FIGURE 47

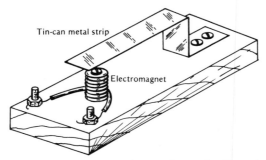

Tin-can metal strip

Electromagnet

Electromagnetic sounder similar to the first telegraph sounder.

FIGURE 48

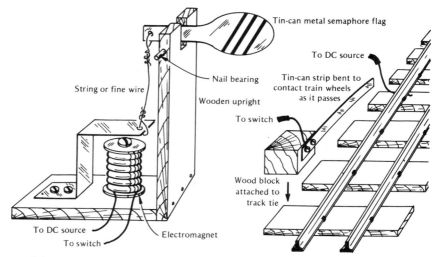

Model railroad semaphore signal and simple track switch.

ment, this device can be made to work quite reliably. A simple switch, activated by the model train, is also shown in the figure and completes the project. Every time the train passes the switch, the metal strip contacts the train wheels, completing the circuit and activating the semaphore.

FIGURE 49

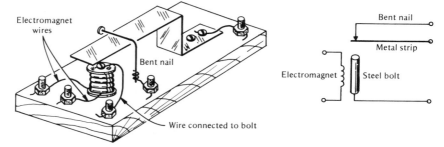

Homemade electromagnetic relay and schematic drawing explaining its operation.

FIGURE 50

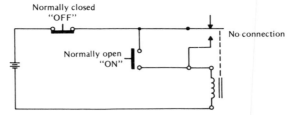

Normally closed
"OFF"

No connection

Normally open
"ON"

"Latching relay" circuit. Other sets of contacts on the relay are used to control the auxiliary circuits.

Returning to the basic electromagnet and metal strip, figure 49 shows another interesting use. A bent nail is arranged as shown, so that it contacts the strip when the magnet is de-energized. The strip then contacts the bolt when the winding is energized. This device is called an electromagnetic relay and works in the same manner as the unit described in figure 44. When energized, one circuit is completed and when de-energized, another one is completed and the first one broken. Commercial relays operate in exactly the same manner and can have several sets of contacts operated by a single electromagnet. In addition, relatively low power electromagnets can operate heavy contacts, thereby allowing large currents to be controlled with small switches. Relays are also used to produce special control functions such as the one shown in figure 50. In this example, two pushbutton switches are arranged, one as a normally open button, and the other as a normally closed button. Pushing the "on" button causes the metal contact strip to

FIGURE 51

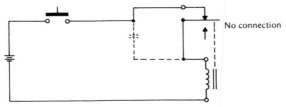

No connection

Connecting the relay to form a buzzer. The dotted lines show the place to connect the capacitor described in the text.

MAGNETISM AND ELECTROMAGNETS

FIGURE 52

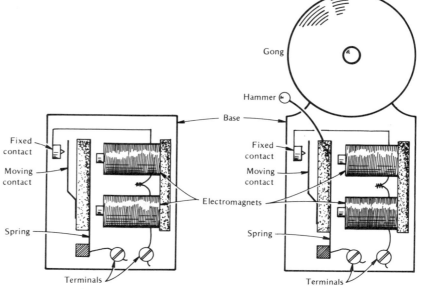

Comparison of a buzzer and a common bell.

pull in, completing the circuit and "latching" the relay. Pushing the "off" button "delatches" the relay. Such a circuit is quite often used in industrial devices, such as elevator controls, cranes, derricks, and even toasters. In these applications, the operator pushes a button (the "on" button in our example) and after the elevator or crane moves, or the toaster reaches the right temperature, the "off" button is pushed, often automatically, turning the system off.

By rearranging the wiring of the relay another common device can be realized. If you connect the circuit of figure 51, you will find that you have produced a buzzer. As current flows through the electromagnet, the metal strip is pulled away from the contact. As soon as the circuit is broken, the magnetic energy disappears and the strip springs back. Now the circuit is reconnected and the process reverses. This buzzer, while identical in principle to commercial units, has one major shortcoming. You will notice a spark produced at the contact as it is opening and closing. Quite a bit of energy is being produced at this spark, with the result that excessive wear is created and the buzzer will soon fail. To remedy this, a device called a capacitor must be connected across the contacts to absorb this energy. While a discussion of the operation of this device is beyond the scope of this book, a 0.01-, 0.05-, or 0.1-microfarad 500-volt disk capacitor should be purchased and installed if you plan to use the buzzer for any period of time. Commercial buzzers utilize special metal contacts that do not wear and therefore do not usually require these capacitors.

From the buzzer to the electric bell is a very short step. All that is necessary is to add a short extension to the metal strip and a small gong—and you have a bell. Figure 52 shows the details of a commercial buzzer and bell for comparison purposes. Notice how their internal circuit is exactly the same as our demonstration unit.

If, instead of winding a coil of wire on a metal rod it is wound on a hollow tube, another interesting electromagnetic device is formed. Referring to figure 53, wind three or four layers of paper around a large, thick nail and coat the paper with glue so that you have made a tube that can easily slide around the nail. Now wind 50–75 turns of bell wire around the tube, each turn side-by-side, and in neat, even layers. Do not squeeze the tube to the point where the nail stops sliding. Finally, cover the winding with electrical tape to hold it in place and slide out the nail.

If you now push the nail halfway into the tube and connect the winding to 1 1/2 or 3 volts, you will see the nail suddenly slide into the tube. Such an electromagnet is called a solenoid and may be used to fabricate an interesting electrical lock. Figure 54 shows these details. Actual dimensions are left out because the lock can be as large or small

FIGURE 53

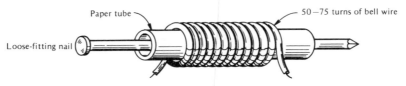

Construction details of a solenoid type of electromagnet.

FIGURE 54

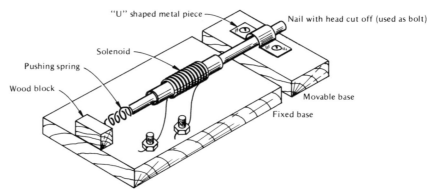

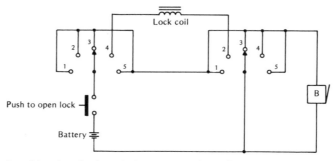

Simple electromagnetic lock. When current flows through the solenoid, the bolt pulls in. When it stops the spring pushes it back into the U-shaped clamp.

as the reader requires. It is only necessary to be sure that the bolt slides very freely in the solenoid tube and that the return spring is just strong enough to do its job. A bit of experimentation may be necessary to get everything working smoothly. A companion "combination" switch for use with the lock is shown in figure 55. By tracing the circuit, you will find that only by switching to the correct position will the lock open. Any other position will sound the alarm.

FIGURE 55

Combination lock switch. Any number of contacts can, of course, be used.

CHAPTER 8

THE ELECTRIC MOTOR

We have just seen how the small movement of a piece of metal near an electromagnet can be employed in many useful ways. We have also seen how, by clever usage of contacts, such motion can be made continuous as in the buzzer. By developing these concepts further, continuous circular motion can be achieved and this is what an American scientist, Thomas Davenport, did in 1835 when he obtained a patent for the world's first electric motor.

To build a demonstration motor, we must first prepare two electromagnets by winding 50 turns of bell wire around two 1/4 × 3-inch stove bolts in the same manner as was used in figure 46. When this is done, connect each winding to its own 1 1/2-volt dry cell and bring the two bolts near each other as shown in figure 56. You will notice that the bolts either attract each other or repel each other, depending on the way the leads are connected. It is this fact that will be used to make our motor. Before disconnecting the coils, carefully note the connections

FIGURE 56

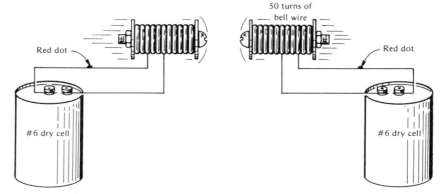

Two electromagnets attract when connected with the proper polarity.

that make the two "heads" of the bolt attract each other by placing a dot of red paint on the wire going to the center terminal (+) of each dry cell.

Referring to figure 57, cut the pieces of tin-can metal and wood as shown for the two electromagnets. Mount the magnets on the supports, as shown in the overall drawing of figure 60. Be certain that the spacing between the two bolts is close to that shown. The final position will be determined later.

To build the armature, refer to figure 58. First obtain a 3/8-inch-diameter wood dowel and drive two 16-gauge wire brads (1 1/2 inches long) into the ends to act as bearings. After checking to make sure the nails are straight, cut off the heads with a hacksaw. Measure the diameter of the bearing nails and drill a hole in each armature support that is

FIGURE 57

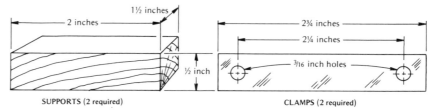

Electromagnet support details.

54

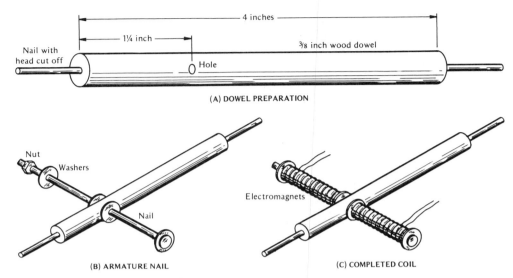

FIGURE 58   *Armature preparation.*

just large enough to accept the nail. There should be no wiggling or looseness to this fit, so do the drilling very carefully. Now drill a hole one-third of the way along the wooden dowel as shown and slide in a 3-inch-long nail that has two washers on the side of the head and two on the other side. Using a hammer, drive a nut on the pointed end of the nail until it is firmly secured. Then file any protruding portion of the point so that it is smooth. Center the nail in the dowel as accurately as you can and glue all washers and the nail in position as shown. When the glue dries completely, wind 50 turns of bell wire on each end of the nail in neat, even layers, being certain that you wind both halves in the same direction. After the winding is complete, arrange both ends of the wire along the dowel and give the coil two coats of varnish or shellac to hold everything in place.

We must now make the commutator, or "moving contacts," for our motor. Referring to figure 59, cut a 1/2-inch-wide strip of aluminum foil just long enough to wrap around the dowel, leaving a gap of 1/32 of an

FIGURE 59

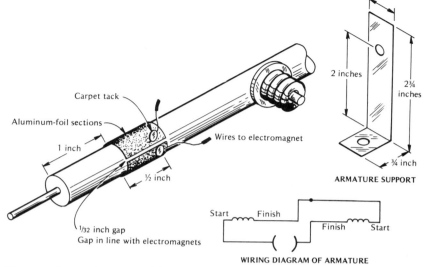

Construction and wiring of the commutator sections. Be sure all wires are
dressed closed to the dowel.

inch between ends. Glue this strip around the dowel one-third of the
way from the end opposite the coil. Be sure the gap is located exactly as
shown in the figure. When the glue dries, carefully cut another 1/32-
inch-wide gap on the exact opposite side of the dowel so that you re-
main with two individual insulated sections. Now strip the ends of the
coil and attach them to the individual sections by means of small carpet
tacks as shown.

At this point, the armature is completed and should be mounted in
its supports, as shown in figure 60. It should also be balanced so that it
will stay in whatever position you put it. If it does not, add a small bit of
modeling clay to the edge of one side of the coil or the other, until
balance occurs. Also, adjust the two electromagnets so that they come
as close to the armature nails as possible, but do not touch. About 1/32
to 1/16 of an inch is desirable. When the armature is now pushed, it
should spin freely.

All that remains is to cut the two thin contacting strips (or brushes,
as they are called) shown in figure 61 and arrange them so that they

FIGURE 60

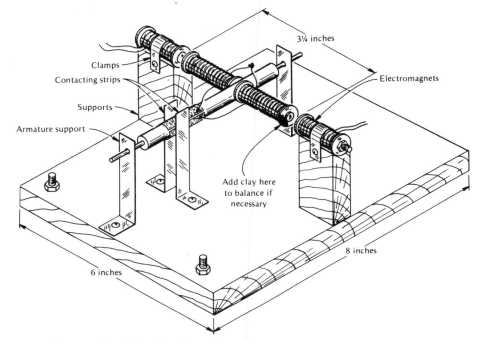

Clamps

Contacting strips

Supports

Armature support

3¼ inches

Electromagnets

Add clay here
to balance if
necessary

8 inches

6 inches

Overall assembly of the electric motor.

gently press on the aluminum-foil contact sections. Figure 61 shows this arrangement as well as the final wiring.

When you have completed all of the previous steps, you are ready to try out the motor. Before doing so, examine the commutator and be certain that the brushes are making good contact with the aluminum-foil strips.

Now connect 3 volts of dry-cell power to the motor, give it a slight "start" with your fingers, and it should whirl merrily along. If you have any problem, examine the brushes and commutator to be certain that they are aligned properly. This is the most critical part of the motor.

What is happening in our demonstration motor is exactly what happens in a commercial electric motor. The fixed electromagnets, called the *field,* attract a moving armature that is also an electromagnet. As soon as the armature magnet moves near the field magnet, the elec-

FIGURE 61

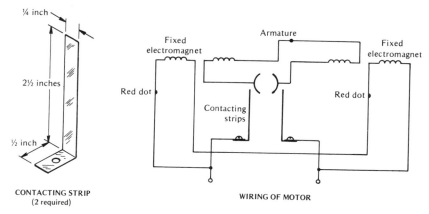

Contacting strip and overall motor wiring diagram.

tric current is reversed, reversing the magnetic field of the armature, and the armature is pushed away toward the other field magnet. Then the process reverses.

Instead of just two sections, commercial motors may have eight to twenty-four or more sections. Also, the field magnets may be of the permanent, nonelectric type such as the ones used in toys. In any event, our simple motor uses the same principles as the motors that are used to operate our modern world. Whether to lift you in an elevator, cool you by a room air conditioner, or help you drill holes with an electric drill, the same magnets, commutator, and brushes are hard at work producing powerful rotary energy from electrical energy.

CHAPTER 9

ALARMS

The experimenter who has a working knowledge of batteries, buzzers, bells, and switches can easily build a wide range of alarm-type devices. These alarms can be used for protection against intruders, announcing devices to indicate when a person passes a particular point, or as safety devices to keep young children out of dangerous locations. In all cases, the basis of operation is the same. A circuit is either made or broken to sound the alarm.

The circuit for the simplest alarm possible is shown in figure 62. Also shown are the construction details of a switch that can be used quite successfully with it. The switch, you will notice, is made of two strips of tin-can metal separated by a thin plastic or varnished cardboard card. Attached to the card is a black thread that is long enough to pass across the area to be protected. If the thread, for example, were strung across a doorway, and the switch mounted to the frame of the doorway, as shown in figure 63, anyone touching the thread would pull the card

FIGURE 62

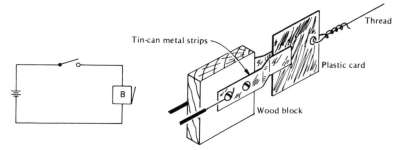

Tin-can metal strips

Thread

Plastic card

B

Wood block

The simplest burglar alarm that can be built.

from between the contacts, complete the circuit, and set off the alarm.

The same scheme can be extended to a window, hallway, staircase, etc. It is only necessary to use a thread that is strong enough not to break when it is disturbed and thin enough to be hard to see.

While this simple alarm is fine for experimental and demonstration purposes, serious systems must employ a different circuit. This is because the easiest sensors to build are those that break a circuit rather than those that complete one, as our card sensor does. Figure 64 shows some sensors (that break a circuit) that can be easily made by the experimenter. They may be used for doors, windows, and even heavy objects. Other variations for specific applications can be easily devised by the experimenter with a little imagination. Most commercially available burglar alarm sensors, incidentally, are of the circuit-breaking type.

The circuit that is employed with this type of sensor is shown in figure 65. It consists of a low-current electromagnetic relay that is always kept engaged and a continuous "alarm loop" that has all of the sensors connected in series. If any sensor opens, the relay drops out, sounding the alarm. If you examine the circuit closely, you will also notice that when the relay does drop out, it cannot be reset unless the "reset" pushbutton switch is pressed. The "off" position of the "operate" switch is, of course, used to prolong battery life when not using the alarm.

The relay that is employed in the alarm must operate with as little

FIGURE 63

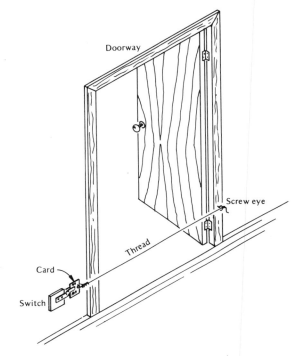

How to install the burglar alarm switch.

current as possible. Since it is always pulled in when the alarm is set, it continually draws current from the battery. If much more than 0.015 amperes is required, very poor battery life will result. Most of the local electrical or electronic supply shops have suitable relays available for low cost. One readily available commercial unit only requires 0.01 amperes at 6 volts. If you have a problem locating this unit, you might wish to check with a local company that installs and maintains burglar alarms. By mounting the batteries, switches, and bell in a neat wooden box, the average experimenter can easily build a complete home security system for a tiny fraction of the cost of a commercial equivalent. Homemade sensors can be employed with this system; however, com-

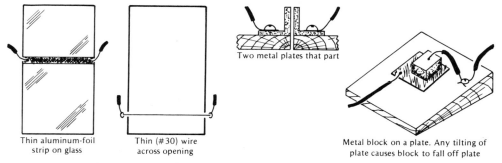

Thin aluminum-foil strip on glass	Thin (#30) wire across opening	Metal block on a plate. Any tilting of plate causes block to fall off plate

FIGURE 64   *Some sensors that break a circuit.*

mercial sensors can certainly be used if desired. Furthermore, if inexpensive thermostats or temperature-operated switches (of the normally closed variety) are used, the system can be easily extended into a useful firealarm circuit as well. Simply add as many sensors as you wish in series.

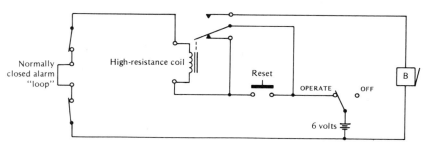

FIGURE 65   *Closed-circuit burglar alarm.*

CHAPTER 10
FuN aNd GAMES

If you have built the various projects and performed the various experiments throughout the past nine chapters, you should have a good idea of what electricity is all about. By utilizing this knowledge and some lamps, buzzers, switches, etc., you can build games and puzzles that will amuse you, mystify some of your friends, and become the basis for carnival attractions when your school or club conducts a fair.

Figure 66 is a simple test of skill called "steady hand" that never fails to amaze. As you can see from the drawing, an irregular length of wire is arranged on two wooden supports and connected in series with a buzzer, battery, and "wand." The idea of the device is to move the wand from one insulated section to the other without sounding the buzzer. It is much harder than you think! Construction details are left to the experimenter, since final size is purely a matter of preference. Assembly should be straight-forward. The buzzer can be any low-voltage doorbell type and the wire, aluminum "ground wire," both of which

FIGURE 66

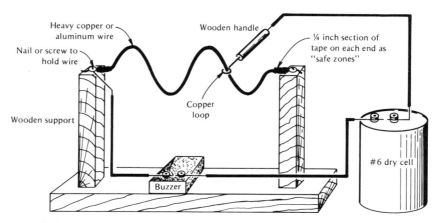

Heavy copper or aluminum wire

Wooden handle

¼ inch section of tape on each end as "safe zones"

Nail or screw to hold wire

Copper loop

Wooden support

#6 dry cell

Buzzer

"Steady hand" test of skill.

should be readily available at your local hardware store for very little cost. The final shape of the wire is also left to the imagination of the builder, although the aluminum wire is very flexible and can be easily changed to make the tester easier or harder, as required.

An equally simple game is the one shown in figure 67. This is an adaptation of a famous New York/Atlantic City Boardwalk game called "Pokerino." The object of the game is to roll five balls down the ramp and light various combinations of lamps that represent playing cards. Scoring is done by the number of similar "cards" obtained in one "hand," much like poker.

The circuit of this game should be quite obvious to the builder. It consists of 16 lamps, ball switches, and a common battery in the series–parallel combination of figure 68. Details of the tin-can metal ball switch, frame, and lamp indicator panel are given in figure 69. The balls should be fairly heavy; the ideal choice is the solid rubber type used for playing handball. Alternately, ordinary rubber balls may be used, but the dimensions of the holes in the playing field will then have to change. The sizes given are similar to the actual professional game and should be followed for best results. If you do a neat job and paint and

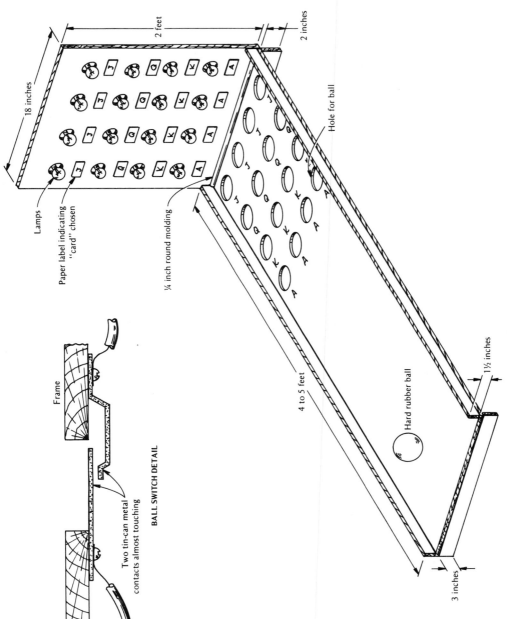

18 inches

2 feet

2 inches

Lamps

Paper label indicating "card" chosen

¼ inch round molding

Hole for ball

Frame

Two tin-can metal contacts almost touching

BALL SWITCH DETAIL

4 to 5 feet

Hard rubber ball

1½ inches

3 inches

FIGURE 67 *Pokerino game. When in use the ball should be slowly rolled towards the hole.*

FIGURE 68

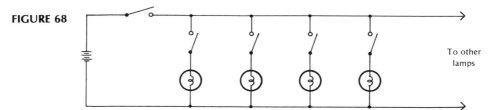

The schematic diagram of Pokerino.

varnish the wood carefully, a very professional unit will result. When using the game, arrange the ramp so that the back is 1 inch lower than the front.

Another test of skill is the device shown in figure 70. The object here is to determine which of two players reacts faster. At the sound of a clap, "ready–set–go," or similar noise, each participant pushes his or her

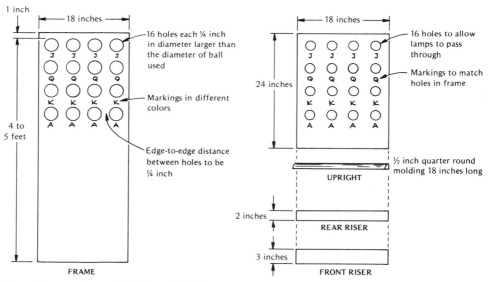

FIGURE 69 *Construction details for Pokerino.*

FIGURE 70

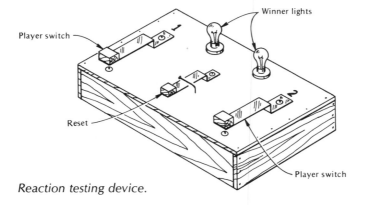

Player switch

Winner lights

Reset

Player switch

Reaction testing device.

button. The faster player lights the appropriate lamp, while the other obtains no indications at all.

The circuit shown in figure 71 utilizes two 6-volt DC relays of the DPDT type. This type of relay has two sets of contacts that are controlled by a single electromagnet. One set is used to hold in the relay and the other to disconnect the opponent's relay. By tracing the path, you will quickly see how the unit works. The reset button is used to start a fresh contest. Figure 72 shows the construction details, although, these may vary according to the needs of the builder. The relays are obtainable from a local electrical parts distributor and should require less than 0.1 ampere at 6 volts for operation. Although the circuit has been designed with 6-volt relays and lamps, 12-volt lamps and relays (and a 12-volt battery) may be substituted with no other changes.

The final unit, shown in figure 73, is an exercise in logic and fancy switching. Four switches are arranged on a panel and labeled as shown. A river is also drawn on the box and an alarm buzzer and light provided. The problem is as follows. A farmer comes to a river with his companions and finds that the only boat he can use to cross the river is just big enough for him and one companion. Since he cannot leave the chicken with the cat, or the chicken with the corn, how can he get everyone and everything across the river safely? The only safe condition

FIGURE 71

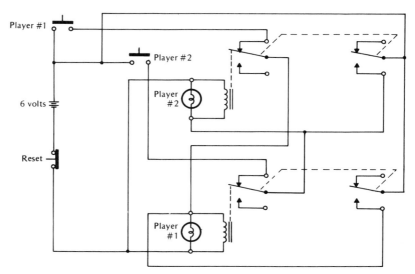

Wiring diagram of reaction tester. Note that the reset switch is normally closed.

is when he is with one of the others, or the cat is alone with the corn. All other conditions are not allowed, as the cat will attack the chicken and the chicken will eat the corn.

Figure 74 shows the circuit and, if you trace it carefully, you will note that the alarm will sound with any incorrect movement of switches. The switches actually used are called "toggle" switches and are available at most electrical supply shops and some hardware stores. Be sure to use the SPDT styles for the farmer, cat, and corn, and the DPDT style for the chicken. Construction details are given in figure 74 and wiring should pose no problem. Be very careful when wiring, however. Make sure that the switches are connected properly.

Utilizing the techniques and simple circuitry required for these games and puzzles will show you just what an electrical experimenter can accomplish in the way of entertaining devices.

It is heartily recommended that all of the various projects in this

FIGURE 72

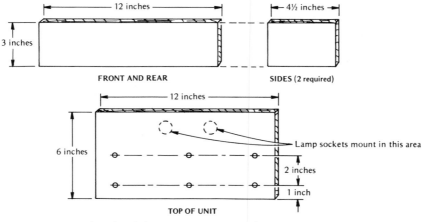

Construction details of the reaction tester cabinet.

FIGURE 73

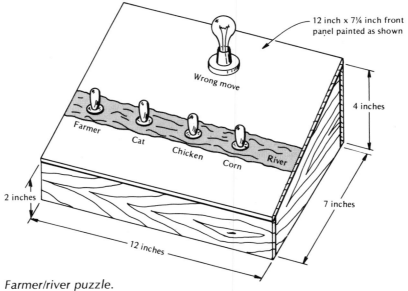

Farmer/river puzzle.

FIGURE 74

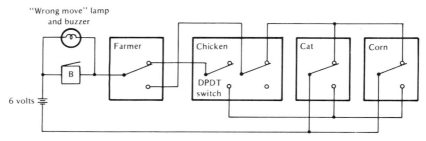

Schematic diagram of puzzle. All switches are SPDT toggle switches except for the "chicken," which is DPDT.

book be used, not only for their own purposes, but as building blocks for other devices. The variations or combinations are limited only by the imagination of the builder.

These projects and experiments might lead some readers to become truly interested in the science of electricity; thus, a fascinating hobby might become a rewarding career. If not, at least some of the mystery of electricity will have been explained.

for further reading

Beginners Level

Electricity and Electronics by Howard Gerrish (South Holland, Ill.: Goodheart-Wilcox)

How Did We Find Out About Electricity by Isaac Asimov (New York: Walker, 1973)

Intermediate Level

Electronics for Young Experimenters by W. E. Pierce (London: G. Bell & Sons, 1966)

First Book of Radio and Electronics by Alfred Morgan (New York: Scribners, 1977)

Junior Science Book of Electricity by Rocco Feravolo (New Canaan, CT: Garrard, 1960)

General Level

Basic Electricity by Milton Kaufman and J. A. Wilson (New York: McGraw Hill, 1973)

Basic Electronics by Bernard Grob (New York: McGraw Hill, 1959)
Introduction to Electronics by Robert Hughes and Peter Pipe (New York: Doubleday, 1961)

Advanced Level

Electronics for Everybody by Ronald Benrey (New York: Harper and Row, 1970)

Periodicals

Popular Electronics (Ziff-Davis, One Park Avenue, New York, N.Y. 10016)
Radio Electronics (Gernsback Publications, 200 Park Avenue South, New York, N.Y. 10017)

index

AC. See Alternating current
"Alarm loop", 60
Alarms, 59-62
   basic principles of, 59-60
   burglar, 60, 61
   circuit for, 59-60
   commercial, 61, 62
Alternating current (AC), 13-14
   power line, 15
   power supply, building an, 22-23
Aluminum wire, 63-64
Amber, 1
   and fur experiment, 1
Amperes, 8
Armature, 26, 27
   building an, 54-56

Batteries, 3, 8-12
   automobile, in emergency lighting, 45
   dry cell, 15
   Galvani's, 3
   in series, 19
   simple, 3, 5
   types of, 11-12, 15-16

varying voltage and current in, 17-20
   Volta's, 5
Bell, electric, 51
Binding post, 34
Brushes, 56-57
Burglar alarms, 60-61
Buzzer, 50, 63-64

Capacitor, 50, 51
Card sensor, 59-60
Circuit, 8
   in an alarm, 59-60, 62
   construction of a, 9-10
   DPDT type, 67
   electric, 8-9
   "latching relay", 49-50
   series-parallel, 43
   simple electric, 8-9
Coil, primary and secondary, 22
Comb and flannel, 2
Commutator, 55-56, 57
Compass
   in a current detector, 3-5, 12-13
   indicator, 24

Conductor, 9-11
  water as a, 11
Connecting wires, 31-33
Current, electric, 2, 3, 7-9
  for experiments, 20-22
  producing a, 12-14
Current scale, calibration of, 29-30
Current sensor, construction of, 26-27

Davenport, Thomas, 53
DC. See Direct current
Detector, current, 3-5, 12-13
Direct current (DC), 13-14
  power supply, 20-21
Dollhouse project, 40-41
DPDT circuit, 68

Edison, Thomas, 40
Electric
  bell, 51
  circuit, 8-10, 43, 49-50, 59-60, 62, 67
  current, 2-3, 7-9, 12-14, 20-22
  energy, 12
  light, 38-39
  motor, 6, 53-62
  pressure, 8
Electrical lock, 51-52
Electrical measuring instruments, 24-30
Electrical tape, 33
Electricity
  basics of, 7-14
  flow of, 7
  history of, 1-6
  measuring, 24-30
  sources of, 15-23
  tools of the trade for, 31-36
  water pipe analogy, 7-8, 17
  what is, 1-6
Electromagnet, 46-52
  in a buzzer, 50-51
  in a DPDT circuit, 67
  fixed, 57
  principle of, 46
Electromagnetic relay, 49-50
  in alarms, 60-61
  in a bell, 51
  in a buzzer, 50
  in a lock, 51-52
Electromagnetic sounder, 47
Electrons, 2
"Elektron", 1
Energy
  chemical, 37

  conversion of, 37
  electrical, 12
  electrical to magnetic, 46
  heat, 37-38

Faraday, Michael, 5
  magnetism experiment, 5-6
Field, 57
Filament, 40
File, flat, 36
Fire alarm circuit, 62
"Form block", 27
Frog, leg muscles of a, 3
Fun and games, 63-70

Galvani, Luigi, 2-3
Game, "Pokerino", 64
  "River-Crossing", 67-68
Games, construction of, 63-70
Generator
  large power, 14
  principles of, 6
  simple, 12-14
Generator coil, 12

Heat energy, 37-38
Heaters, 38-39
"Heating element", 38

Indicator
  compass, 24, 25-28
  voltage/current, 12-13
"Input coil", primary, 22
Insulation, 31-33
Insulator, 9-10

Lamp
  assemblies in emergency lighting, 43-45
  brass base for a, 40
  building a, 41-42
  in circuit, 43
  miniature, 42-43
Lemon battery, 4-5
Light bulb
  Edison's first practical, 40
  incandescent, 40
Lighting fixtures
  installing and wiring, 42-43
  types of, 40-41
Lighting system, emergency, 43-45
Lock, electrical, 51-52

Magnet, bar, 12

Magnetic energy, 12, 13
Magnetic field, 6, 22
Magnetism, 46-52
  relationship to, 5-6
Metal strip, 47, 48, 49
Model railroad semaphore, 47-48
Morse, Samuel, 47
Motor, electric, 6, 53-62
  building a, 53-54
  a commercial, 58
"Moving contacts", 55-56

Nichrome, 38

Oersted, Hans Christian, 5
Ohm, Georg Simon, 25
Ohms, 25
Ohm's law, 25
"Output coil", secondary, 22

Parallel circuit, 17
Pioneers, 1-6
Pliers, 36
"Pokerino" game, 64
Power and light, 37-45
Power supply, building a
  AC, 22-23
  DC, 20-21
Pressure, electric, 8
Puzzle, "River-Crossing", 67-68

"Quick connect", post, 34

Reaction tester, 66-67
Reflectors, flashlight, 45
Relay
  commercial, 49
  electromagnetic, 44, 49, 50-52, 60-61
"Reset" pushbutton, 60
Resistance, 25, 37-38
"River-Crossing" puzzle, 67-68

Scissors, 36
Screwdriver, 36
Sensor, 44
  circuit-breaker, 59-60
  commercial, 61-62

in emergency lighting system, 44
SPDT, 44
Series circuit, 19
  and parallel, 43
Snips, tin, 36
Soldering, 41-42
Solenoid, 51-52
SPDT
  electromagnetic relay, 44
  sensor, 68
Speed of response, 66-67
Static electricity, 1-3
"Steady Hand" test of skill, 63
Switches
  in series-parallel circuit, 43
  types of, 33, 68

Tape, electrical, 33, 36
Telegraph, 47
Terminals, 4
Tester, 24
  reaction, 66-67
Test of skill, "Steady Hand", 63
Thales of Miletus, 1
"Toggle" switches, 68
Tools, recommended, 31-36
Transformer
  principles of, 6, 22
  purchase of, 23
Tungsten, 40

volt, 3, 8
Volta, Allesandro, 3
Voltage/current indicator, 12-13
Voltage sensor, 26
Voltmeter, calibration of, 28-29
Volt-ohm-meter (V-O-M), 30

Watt, James, 37
Watts, 37-38
Wire
  bell, 45
  connecting, 31-33
  copper, 31
  high resistance, 38
"Wire nuts", 33-34
Wire strippers, 36